S0-DPD-997

Presented to

....

by

....

on

....

Copyright © 2014 Lion Hudson/
Tim Dowley Associates

All rights reserved. No part of this publication may be
reproduced or transmitted in any form or by any means,
electronic or mechanical, including photocopy, recording,
or any information storage and retrieval system,
without permission in writing from the publisher.

Published by Candle Books
an imprint of
Lion Hudson plc
Wilkinson House, Jordan Hill Road,
Oxford OX2 8DR, England
www.lionhudson.com/candle

ISBN 978 1 85985 952 0
e-ISBN 978 1 78128 120 8

First edition 2014

Acknowledgments
All scripture quotations, except those listed below, are taken or adapted
from the Contemporary English Version. Copyright © 1991, 1992, 1995
by American Bible Society. Used by permission.

Scripture quotations on pages 6, 9, 16, and 60 are taken from the Holy Bible,
New Living Translation, copyright © 1996, 2004, 2007 by Tyndale House Foundation.
Used by permission of Tyndale House Publishers, Inc., Carol Stream, Illinois 60188.
All rights reserved.

A catalogue record for this book is available
from the British Library

Printed and bound in China,
November 2013, LH17

Blessings
for
Little Girls

Compiled by Juliet David
Illustrated by Julie Clay

CANDLE
BOOKS

This collection of age-appropriate Bible verses
has been specially designed for beginning readers.

Promises, sayings, and simple truths that speak
clearly to young minds have been carefully
selected from Scripture.

Some of the best-known and most-loved
Bible verses are included.

Most are simple enough to repeat and memorize.

Many can be used as simple prayers.

This book offers first steps in a lifetime's
walk through the Bible.

J.D.

The Lord is my shepherd;
I have everything I need.

PSALM 23:1

The earth is the Lord's,
and everything in it.

PSALM 24:1

I asked the Lord for help,
and he saved me
from all my fears.

PSALM 34:4

Tell the Lord how thankful you are,
because he is kind
and always merciful.

PSALM 118:1

I praise the Lord
for answering my prayers
and saving me.

PSALM 118:21

Lord, you are mine!
I promise to obey your words!

PSALM 119:57

I lie awake at night,
thinking of your promises, Lord.

PSALM 119:148

Always let God lead you,
and he will clear the road
for you to follow.

PROVERBS 3:6

Don't be afraid.
I am with you…
I am your God.

ISAIAH 41:10

Tell the whole world to sing
a new song to the Lord!

ISAIAH 42:10

God said,
"I have rescued you.
I have called you by name;
now you belong to me."

ISAIAH 43:1

God said,
"I am your Creator.
You were in my care
even before you were born."

ISAIAH 44:2

Good news! You're saved…
Your God is now King.

ISAIAH 52:7

Turn to the Lord!
He can still be found.
Call out to God!
He is near.

ISAIAH 55:6

Everyone who asks will receive.

MATTHEW 7:8

Make your light shine,
so others will see the good you do
and will praise
your Father in heaven.

MATTHEW 5:16

Jesus said,
"If you are tired…
come to me
and I will give you rest."

MATTHEW 11:28

God will bless you people
who are now crying.
You will laugh!

LUKE 6:21

Jesus said,
"Love your enemies
and be good to them."

LUKE 6:35

Jesus said,
"You will never get into God's kingdom
unless you enter
like a little child!"

LUKE 18:17

God loved the people of this world
so much that he gave his only Son,
so that everyone who believes in him
will have eternal life.

JOHN 3:16

Jesus said,
"I am the bread that gives life!
No one who comes to me
will ever be hungry."

JOHN 6:35

Jesus said,
"I am the light for the world!
Follow me,
and you won't be
walking in the dark."

JOHN 8:12

Jesus said,
"I am the good shepherd.
I know my sheep,
and they know me."

JOHN 10:14

Jesus said,
"I am the way, the truth,
and the life! Without me,
no one can go to the Father."

JOHN 14:6

Jesus said,
"Love each other,
as I have loved you."

JOHN 15:12

God will bless you
in everything you do,
if you listen and obey,
and don't just hear and forget.

JAMES 1:25

Draw close to God,
and God will draw close to you.

JAMES 4:8

God cares for you,
so turn all your worries
over to him.

I PETER 5:7